BRIDGETON, N. J. 08302

THAILAND
Land of the White Elephant

1997-98 NWMS READING BOOKS

RESOURCE BOOK FOR THE LEADER

IMAGINE THE POSSIBILITIES
Edited by Beverlee Borbe

FOR THE READER

BY GRACE TRANSFORMED
God at Work in Brazil
By Tim Crutcher

ONLY ONE LIFE . . .
The Autobiography of Lorraine O. Schultz
By Lorraine O. Schultz with C. Ellen Watts

JESUS WILL REPAY
By Becky Hancock

THAILAND: LAND OF THE WHITE ELEPHANT
Edited by Jean R. Knox and Michael P. McCarty

TO THE SHELTER
Journeys of Faith in the Middle East
By Kay Browning

WHERE THE RIVER FLOWS
Bringing Life to West Africa
By Linda Seaman

THAILAND

Land of the White Elephant

Edited by
Jean R. Knox
and
Michael P. McCarty

Nazarene Publishing House
Kansas City, Missouri

Copyright 1997
by Nazarene Publishing House

ISBN 083-411-6421

Printed in the
United States of America

Cover design: Mike Walsh

All Scripture quotations are from the *Holy Bible, New International Version*® (NIV®). Copyright © 1973, 1978, 1984 by International Bible Society. Used by permission of Zondervan Publishing House. All rights reserved.

10   9   8   7   6   5   4   3   2   1

To the memory of
George E. Rench
—faithful friend, missionary mentor, inspiring leader.
Under his leadership as the regional director for the
Asia-Pacific Region from 1985 to 1994,
our work in Thailand was begun.

CONTENTS

Pronunciation Guide	8
Foreword	11
Preface	13
1. Beginnings Robert H. Scott	15
2. From *The King and I* to *Thaicom II* Michael P. McCarty	24
3. "To Be Thai Is to Be Buddhist" W. Richard Knox	29
4. Getting Past the Goobledygook Jean R. Knox	36
5. Sowing and Reaping W. Richard Knox	43
6. The Khmer Connection Michael P. McCarty	51
7. The Golden Triangle Eric Kellerer, Samuel Yangmi, and Brent Cobb	60
8. What Do All Those Letters Mean? Eric Kellerer, Paula Kellerer, and Jean R. Knox	68
9. The Church on the Move W. Richard Knox and Michael P. McCarty	76
10. Sacrifices of Praise: Testimonies of Thai Nazarenes	83

Thai Language Pronunciation Guide

The Thai language is written in the Thai script. When it is transliterated into English, numerous variations are possible. Many Thai vowels are absent from English, and Thai contains five speaking tones instead of accents. With those warnings in mind, this guide should allow you to pronounce the Thai names in this book with as much accuracy as can be expected of a non-Thai speaker.

Vowels	Pronunciations
a (or ar)	"ah" as in *father*
ae	"eh" as in *bed*
ai	"I"
aw (or or)	"aw" as in *taught*
ay	long "a" as in *day*
e	"eh" as in *bed*
i (or ee)	"ee" as in *breeze*
o	"oh" as in *oat*
oo (or u)	"oo" as in *food*
uh	"uh" with teeth together
ua	pronounced as two vowels: "oo-ay"

Consonants	Pronunciations
b or bh	"b"
c or j	between hard "c" and "j"
d or dh	"d"
f	"f"

g or k	between hard "g" and "k"
h	"h"
kh	"k"
l	"l" unless final—then "n"
m	"m"
n	"n"
ng	"ng" as in *sing*
p	unaspirated "p"
ph	"p"
r	rolled unless final—then "h"
s	"s" unless final—then "n"
t	unaspirated "t"
th	"t"
v or w	"w"

Foreword

What a fascinating title! What a fascinating book! Nazarenes really will enjoy reading this one. It contains the success story of modern missions. The commitment, sacrifices, and demands are not a great deal different from those in accounts from other pioneer missionary endeavors. This one does reflect the result of adequate preparation and adaptation of methods and tools that have been effectively used elsewhere and have provided the foundation for "doing it right."

Credit, of course, goes first to God, who inspired, directed, and led right from the beginning. Then there are the missionaries—so bright, so well educated, and so deeply dedicated to the fulfillment of their calling. Appreciation must also be expressed to denominational leaders, administrators, and, of course, the entire support system, which includes the smallest local Nazarene World Mission Society (NWMS) chapter in the church. Of special significance in this story is the effectiveness of adequate professional missionary training as presented primarily in Nazarene Theological Seminary classes on missiology.

But this story includes another wonderful dimension. You will read of the tremendous part the Japanese Church of the Nazarene had in this development as well as the strong support given later by the Korean Nazarenes.

It is not an overstatement, then, to say that this book is a modern missionary success treatise. For this a denomination that made a radical decision some years ago to be a distinctly international church must be grateful. And we are!

—*Jerald D. Johnson*
General Superintendent
Church of the Nazarene

Preface

In the days of the absolute monarchy in Thailand, all the albino elephants born in the kingdom were automatically the property of the king. Since the king received many of these baby albino elephants, he began a tradition of using them to honor those who had accomplished great deeds for the kingdom.

In a royal ceremony, the honoree would be brought to the palace and publicly presented with the baby albino elephant. Since the animal needed to be cared for, the honoree would also be given the necessary land on which to maintain it. As a result, the person so honored would become a noble in the kingdom. Thus was born the Order of the White Elephant, the Thai equivalent of knighthood.

However, if the king did not like someone, he could also present that person with a baby albino elephant—only this time no land would be given to care for the elephant. The one receiving this "gift" could not sell it, give it away, permit it to get sick and die, nor use it for any kind of work because it represented the honor of the king. Each year the man would have to provide more and more food to feed the unwanted elephant. We keep that tradition alive today with the giving of "white elephant gifts."

The task of planting the Church of the Nazarene in the Land of the White Elephant is a mammoth one. However, God has given us a good beginning, and this book is a record of that. May the following chapters inspire you to trust the King who has made each of us a "noble" in His kingdom and has given us the task of planting the flag of His kingdom over the many kingdoms on the earth.

I want to express special appreciation to the entire Thailand mission council who had a part in the production of this book and especially my coeditor, Jean Knox, who worked tirelessly from the very beginning days when this book was only a dream. Appreciation is also given to General Superintendent Jerald D. Johnson and Robert H. Scott, former World Mission Division director, under whose leadership the work in Thailand began.

Our task is a gigantic one, which seems to grow bigger year by year. However, our King has given us all the resources we need as we depend upon Him. We would appreciate your prayers for the future work of the Church of the Nazarene in Thailand and for the nations that surround it. Thank you for taking the time to walk with us in the Land of the White Elephant.

—Michael P. McCarty

1
Beginnings

ROBERT H. SCOTT

IT WAS 10:30 P.M. ON JANUARY 12, 1988. The gleaming white Thai International Airways 747 had just touched down in Bangkok, Thailand. I could hardly believe I was actually standing on the soil of that intriguing country. As events would unfold over the next few days, however, I would witness the most specific providential leadership of God and would see His miraculous hand at work in great and gracious ways.

"Thailand" means "land of the free," so named because in earlier centuries it successfully retained its freedom when surrounding countries were colonized by Western powers. It was believed that a special guardian angel named Phra Sayam Devadhiraj had protected the land. Subsequent worship of that spirit has been part of the religious life for many in Thailand.

It was George Rench, then the Asia-Pacific regional director, who first brought Thailand to my attention. In his region, he said, this country remained one of the largest left without a Nazarene church or missionary. He felt deep concern for the more than 50 million people of this constitutional monarchy, over 94 percent of whom followed the religion of Buddhism. Some 4 percent identified themselves as Muslim. A bare 1 percent were classified as Christian, and only 0.3 percent were Evangelical. Thailand, Dr. Rench rightly insisted, was one of the most untouched mission fields of the world.

From all outward appearances, it seemed impossible to anticipate successfully opening Nazarene work in Thailand. In 1982 the government had become concerned about the proliferation of Christian missionaries in the country and decreed that future Christian church work would be limited to groups then registered in the country. The same governmental edict limited the number of missionaries to the number present at that time. Each Christian group in the country then was allowed to number and categorize its personnel according to individual group policies. The result of such action was to set up the equivalent of quota slots that would appear to forever place a cap on both groups and numbers of Christian missionaries to Thailand.

George Rench, however, was a man of great vision and burden for the unreached peoples of the world. He was convinced a way could be found to overcome this obstacle, gain missionary entrance, and begin Nazarene work. His concern for these people and his conviction that Thailand needed the Church of the Nazarene led us to arrange this trip. He was to join me the following day, and we would commence the quest for some means by which our beloved church could come to this special country.

One does not have to stay long in Thailand to feel a special love for this place and these people. There is warmth and friendliness. There is an industriousness and energy. There is variety of culture and lifestyle. There is openness to people from outside the country. And there is spiritual hunger and need!

Approximately one-tenth of the population of Thailand lives in Bangkok, a massive, bustling city unlike much of the rural and hill country of Thailand. The city has the contrast between poverty and opulent wealth that is familiar in many Asian cities. Bangkok is a city of canals, referred to by some in the past as "the Venice of Asia." However, the canals, reaching out from the Chao Phraya River, have become terribly polluted. Though thousands of Bangkok's citizens live along these canals and children play and bathe in them, the pollution offers a sad face, reflecting part of the city's need and desperation.

There are 4,000 Buddhist temples in Bangkok, and they comprise some of its most spectacular sights. On the grounds of the Grand Palace is a solid jade Buddha. Its dramatic lighting takes one's breath away. In another simple temple a few blocks away is a gold Buddha weighing over 5 tons. You are never allowed to forget the Buddhist influence. The Buddhist monks, with their shaved heads and yellow robes, are an ever present part of the people scenery of Thailand.

The day following my arrival, George Rench arrived from the regional office in Manila. The two of us continued previous planning to find a way for

The Temple of the Dawn in Bangkok

Nazarene mission work to open here. Advance research into church registration possibilities had come up with two groups of people we concluded might be helpful. We made appointments to meet with leaders of these groups.

Our first call took us to the office of the Evangelical Fellowship of Thailand (EFT). The EFT served as an umbrella organization for about 50 small Christian groups and was recognized by the Thai government as a spokesperson for these groups. The groups within EFT held 825 of the quota slots for missionary work in Thailand.

Charan Ratanabutra, executive secretary of EFT, welcomed us with open arms. He was most anxious to have a global missionary organization like the Church of the Nazarene in his country. He had invited another Thai ministerial colleague to be present in our meeting. This man, Silawech Kanjanamukda, was the national leader of the Church of God, Anderson, Indiana. He was not familiar with the Church of the Nazarene, but when we explained our Wesleyan theological roots, he was exuberant at the prospects of another Holiness witness for his country. He and Dr. Ratanabutra assured us of every effort possible to assist us.

The easiest way for Nazarenes to enter Thailand, these men explained, would be to find an organization with registered quota slots that were not presently filled and ask for the privilege of occupying those positions. They suggested two organizations for us to visit.

That same afternoon we visited one of these organizations, which also operated an Evangelical Bible school in Bangkok. This impressive group did indeed have one opening, but they had just concluded a tentative arrangement to fill it. They suggested we contact the Asia Christian Mission, located in Chiang Mai, some 400 miles to the north of Bangkok. This was the other organization that had been suggested to us in the EFT office.

We had also heard there was a young man in the Chiang Mai area who had attended MidAmerica Nazarene College in Olathe, Kansas. He was said to be Burmese, doing Christian work in the mountain villages around Chiang Mai. We had been told his name was Samuel Yangmi.

Flying into Chiang Mai, we contacted a young couple who were missionaries with an independent church organization. They knew Samuel Yangmi but did not know his whereabouts on that day. He had an associate, they said, and they would take us to where this person was.

When we knocked on the door of this house, to our surprise a young American answered the knock. When we introduced ourselves, he responded by saying, "I graduated two years ago from Nazarene Theological Seminary in Kansas City." He was there working with Asia Christian Mission, and he reported the present spokesman for that group was none other than Samuel Yangmi. He also said that "Sammy," as he was called, was due to arrive at his house within the hour.

Samuel Yangmi was born in southern China to parents who belonged to the Lisu people. When he was a small baby, his parents migrated to Burma, only to be driven back across the border. In the process, Samuel was given in adoption to a Chinese lady in Burma who was the adopted daughter of American missionaries Rev. and Mrs. J. Russell Morse, who had worked among the Lisu. Their daughter became Samuel's mother and eventually married a Lisu man who also adopted Samuel.

In the political revolution of Burma, Samuel's parents had been forced to leave that country and so immigrated to the United States, where Sammy obtained U.S. citizenship. Through his American family connections he had heard of MidAmerica Nazarene College and had been told they had a study program in agriculture and missions. After his own wedding he went to Olathe, Kansas, and enrolled in the school. While there, his wife, Lumae, was cared for by Nazarene medical doctor Paul Wardlaw, who had shown special Christian interest and compassion and had delivered their first child. Sammy and Lumae were greatly impressed by this Christian doctor and by the Church of the Nazarene.

When Sammy walked in the door of the home and was introduced to us, he expressed great surprise. He said, "For the past two weeks I have had the strongest impression to contact someone in the Church of the Nazarene, and I was not sure how to go about doing that." He proceeded to say that this interest was precipitated by the fact that his organization, Asia Christian Mission, had vacant missionary slots, and his experience with Nazarenes had given him a desire to see those slots filled by Nazarene missionaries and Nazarene mission work. He then looked at us and said, "Now tell me—why are you here?"

We responded that we had come to this remote part of Thailand looking for missionary slots, completely without knowing he was the one who held the key to our quest. There were tears in all of our eyes as we marveled at the amazing providence of God and shared the affirmation that it must indeed be His will and plan for our church to enter the country of Thailand. The following week Sammy Yangmi drove to Bangkok and signed the necessary papers to make the missionary quota slots available to the Church of the Nazarene.

Two days later, leaving Bangkok on a flight to Hong Kong, I found myself seated by a distinguished-looking Thai man. We exchanged names, and I found that he was a deputy governor working for the king of Thailand. On the several-hour flight we had ample opportunity to exchange personal and professional information. Though he was a devout Buddhist, he expressed interest in and appreciation for a global mission organization like the Church of the Nazarene. As we shook hands and said good-bye in Hong Kong, he expressed hope that our church might indeed come to his country and offered any help he might be able to give. I could not help but feel this was another fascinating confirmation that God indeed wanted the Church of the Nazarene in Thailand.

A final confirmation came a few days later as I met with the District Advisory Board of the Japan District Church of the Nazarene in Tokyo. One purpose of our meeting was to decide on the disbursement of the sale proceeds of a valuable piece of land. The property had originally been purchased with Alabaster funds for Nazarene mission use by William Eckel, pioneer missionary to Japan. The purchase price had been very small, but dramatic land value escalation had occurred, and the land was sold for several million United States dollars.

As I reported on my recent Thailand experience, these Japanese Nazarenes were enthusiastic in wishing to help provide funding for opening the work in Thailand. They offered a major portion of the land sale proceeds to set up a trust fund for the early years of our work in Thailand, including payment of missionary salaries and purchase of needed properties. The funding of Thailand Nazarene missions could therefore take place over and above General Budget dollar resources.

So Thailand became another new country for Nazarene mission work. In the years since that late January day, outstanding Nazarene missionaries have spread across the city of Bangkok and the countryside as well. Property has been purchased and buildings erected. Converts have joined the global Nazarene family, and some of these are now ministers helping to carry out our work.

Also in the ministerial corps are Sammy and Lumae Yangmi, who not only gave the first slots for our work to begin but also fell deeply in love with the Church of the Nazarene. In 1993 they requested affiliation with Nazarene world missions and joined Olathe, Kansas, College Church of the Nazarene as their home church. Today they serve under contract with the Nazarene World Mission Division as missionaries in the Church of the Nazarene. The miracles of God go on, and who would be able to tell what the subsequent chapters will unfold?

2
From "The King and I" to "Thaicom II"

MICHAEL P. MCCARTY

IT IS ONE OF THE BETTER-KNOWN scenes from the musical *The King and I*. Powerful King Mongkut of Siam and petite English teacher Anna are in confrontation over the life of a slave. The mighty king wants the man killed. The teacher pleads for mercy. The king finally relents and spares the man's life. Today the movie edition of this story is still officially banned from Thailand, because it depicts the Thai king as weak and easily swayed by the whims of a woman. Both the story and the reaction to it say something about the relationship of Thailand to the Western world, a relationship that has shaped much of its modern history.

The Thai people began their history as migrants in Southeast Asia before the birth of Christ. Some date their history to the new beginning of humanity after a great flood, caused by people's ingratitude to the "Heavenly Spirit," destroyed everyone but three holy chiefs. These migrants formed tribes that came together as kingdoms in the 11th and 12th centuries. Smaller kingdoms within the area of present-day Thailand rose and fell, but the people advanced in culture and trade.

That trade began to include European powers, specifically the Portuguese and the Dutch, in the 1500s. Over the next 200 years the people of Thailand alternated between periods of freedom from their enemies and domination by Burma. Finally the present Chakri dynasty of Thailand was established in 1782 with the coronation of General Chao Phyra Chakri as King Rama I.

King Rama I began his rule of Thailand by strengthening the defense against Burma to the north and by protecting the subject nations of Laos and Cambodia from European domination. As the French advanced in Indochina, Rama III forged an alliance with Britain, thus establishing closer ties with the West without surrendering his kingdom's independence.

This dance between independence and the Western colonial powers continued to dominate Thai history. King Mongkut (Rama IV) had been an abbot of a Buddhist monastery for 20 years when his brother died, and he was propelled into the kingship of what was then known by the West as Siam.

Reigning from 1851 to 1868, King Mongkut was a pen pal of President Abraham Lincoln and even offered to send some elephants to his American friend if Lincoln thought they would help in his winning the Civil War. He was a learned man with a keen sense of political balance that kept Thailand free of any European colonial rule. He afforded his son, Crown Prince Chulalongkorn, a superb education that combined the best of both traditional Thai and Western elements. This helped to pave the way for King Chulalongkorn (Rama V) to lead his nation into the modern world of the 20th century.

During the reign of Chulalongkorn, slavery was abolished, the judiciary was reformed, a modern army was created, and education was revamped. In addition, the monarchy was strengthened, revenue collection and government control was centralized, the internal government leadership structure was improved, and the present borders of Thailand were clearly defined. The king became more publicly identified with his subjects and, consequently, more open to criticism by them. When King Chulalongkorn died October 24, 1910, having reigned for 42 years, a dynamic new modernized state had been created.

Chulalongkorn's son Vajiravudh (Rama VI) led Thailand into World War I on the side of the Allies, sending 1,300 men to France to assist in the war effort. Upon his death in 1925, his brother Prajadhipok (Rama VII), the 76th child born to King Chulalongkorn, ascended the throne.

Prajadhipok was to be the last of Thailand's absolute monarchs. Because of famine and the Great Depression, the military took over the government in 1932, though they invited Prajadhipok back as a constitutional monarch. From this point on the military became a dominating force in Thai politics and society.

With the military in power, Thailand regained some of the territories in Laos and Cambodia that it had previously relinquished to France. However, in 1941 Japan invaded Thailand on the same day it attacked Pearl Harbor. The military leaders of Thailand chose to permit the Japanese free passage rights in exchange for Thai independence. However, an anti-Japanese underground arose; and when the war was over, Thailand was allowed to join the newly formed United Nations if they would only give up the territory they had recaptured from the French.

At the end of World War II the young Ananda Mahidol returned to Thailand to be crowned King Rama VIII. Unfortunately, he was assassinated, and his brother, Bhumibol Mahidol, was chosen to take his place on the throne as Rama IX. With the advance of Communism in Southeast Asia in the 1960s and '70s, Thailand joined with the United States and other nations to combat it.

Although the Vietnam War ended in 1975, the influence of the West on Thailand has steadily increased. Bangkok has become a megacity of 10 million residents, transient workers, and ever present tourists, which number more than 5½ million each year. The streets of the capital are overshadowed by an ever increasing number of huge skyscrapers. Multitudes of Thai handicrafts can be found for sale as well as a growing number of American fast-food restaurants, which have become the favorites of the younger Thai generations.

While agriculture continues to be the major industry in the kingdom (Thailand is the world's second-largest exporter of rice), manufacturing, banking, telecommunications, and tourism are now major players. Stock market activity is noted daily,

Thai banks are found throughout the world, the kingdom has become the gem capital of the world, and two Thai-owned telecommunication satellites, proudly known as *Thaicom I* and *Thaicom II*, are presently orbiting overhead.

King Rama IX celebrated 50 years as king of Thailand on June 9, 1996. Although the nation has struggled to come of age in the modern world, their monarch represents the bridge between the kingdom's heritage and the rapidly changing world. He has held his people steady through many rough seas over the past 50 years, and he is greatly loved by all. Born in Boston, King Bhumibol represents the culmination of an amazing history of growth and development for the people called Thai during the past 2,000 years. And we join in their celebration.

3
"To Be Thai Is to Be Buddhist"

W. Richard Knox

IT IS LOCATED AT THE Temple of the Emerald Buddha at the Grand Palace next to the Chao Phraya River in downtown Bangkok, and it is the most sacred image in all of Thai Buddhism. The Emerald Buddha is a statue of Buddha carved from one piece of jade about two feet high. It sits up high on an altar designed to represent the traditional chariots attributed to Hindu gods. The statue was discovered in northern Thailand in the 15th century and was finally brought to Bangkok in the late 1700s.

Visitors are required to take off their shoes before entering the chapel to see the Emerald Buddha and to sit on the floor with their feet facing away from the Buddha image. The Thai people, with their hands folded in front of them, bow with their face to the floor three times. As they bow, they say, "I take refuge in the Buddha. I take refuge in the dharma [Buddha's teachings]. I take refuge in the sangha [Buddhist monkhood]."

Thai Buddhists in worship

"To be Thai is to be Buddhist," as they say in Thailand, and it is very near the truth. Thailand is the most solidly Buddhist country in the world, with over 94 percent of the population adhering to that religion. One of the many titles for the king of Thailand is "Protector of Buddhism." Though freedom of religion is guaranteed by the constitution, Buddhism is the official religion by law. In Thailand, Buddhism is more than just another religion or even the main religion. Buddhist elements permeate the entire culture and the worldview of the Thai people.

The founder of Buddhism was Siddhartha Gautama, a Hindu prince who lived in northern India in the sixth century B.C. He was raised in a life of luxury in a palace. At the age of 29 he left his family and the life of ease to go in search of a solution to the problem of the suffering of mankind. Seated under the bodhi tree, Gautama attained enlightenment and became the Buddha, which means "the Enlightened One." Buddha did not claim to be a god or to have received any inspiration or revelation from any god. He was a man who found the way and then taught others how to find the way for themselves.

Buddha's teachings are summarized in his first sermon on "The Four Noble Truths." The four truths are (1) All of life is suffering; (2) The cause of suffering is desire; (3) The cure for suffering is the extinction of desire; (4) The way to extinguish desire is the Eightfold Path. That path consists of right understanding, right thought, right speech, right action, right means of livelihood, right effort, right mindfulness, and right concentration.

The path that the Buddha taught consists entirely of human endeavor and human effort. According to Buddha, people are their own masters. Each person must work out his or her own salvation through personal effort and intelligence.

As a result of this teaching, there is no God in Theravada Buddhism (the form of Buddhism in Thailand). Because there is no God, there is no supernatural power to help people in their daily lives or to forgive and save them. There is no power to change them or to change their world. As a result, many Thais are searching in many different places for a power to help them—in Hinduism, astrology, ancestor worship, and animism.

On the corner next to the Hyatt Regency Hotel in Bangkok is the Erawan Shrine. In the middle of the shrine is a large four-faced bronze statue of Brahma, the creator god in Hinduism. Many people come to kneel at the shrine and offer flowers, food, candles, and incense at the altar before the statue.

Other Thais seek supernatural power through astrology. It is not unusual for people to go to a Buddhist monk to ask for a lucky number for the winning lottery ticket. Important government and business events and decisions, as well as the dates for weddings and ordinations into the monkhood, are based on horoscopes and the star charts.

The Chinese Thai also add ancestor worship to their search for supernatural power. On special days, the Chinese Thais burn special money or paper cars or houses to send to their relatives in the spirit world. This is done to try to appease the ancestral spirits and enlist their aid.

Other Thais seek supernatural power through interaction with spirits. Many people wear white string around their wrists to protect themselves from the evil spirits. Men have tattoos for the same reason. In front of most homes and businesses in Thailand are spirit houses, where flower and food offerings are left. People hope the spirits will live in these houses and not trouble them in their homes or businesses.

In addition to the fact that there is no God in Buddhism, there are some other concepts that sound strange to the Westerner but are an important part of the Hindu/Buddhist worldview. These are the ideas of *karma*, *merit*, and *reincarnation*.

Karma is the accumulation of all the good and bad things a person has ever done—in this life and in previous lives. A person's status in life depends upon his or her karma. Good deeds must be performed in order to earn *merit* so that a person's next life cycle is better than this one.

Reincarnation is the belief that people are reborn on this earth after they die. The Buddha said he remembered 550 of his previous lives. I asked a Thai man one day, "If it took Buddha 550 lives to reach enlightenment, how many times is it going to take you?" He answered, "50,000." So the only hope that a Thai Buddhist has is to do some good deeds to try to earn merit—like giving food to the monks, giving money to the temple, helping a person in need—so that his next life cycle is higher than the present one. And he must do this over and over and over again—50,000 times.

Because there is no God in Buddhism, there is no forgiveness from sin. So when a Thai Buddhist violates the ethical rules of his religion, there is no one to whom he can turn for help. The only option he has is to do some good deeds to counteract the bad deeds. Without forgiveness, a person must earn merit to try to counterbalance sins committed.

Thus, the Thai people feel they are trapped in a seemingly eternal cycle of karma with no way out. I have never met a Thai who felt he had a chance of reaching the end of the cycle, called *nirvana*. But Thais know no other way to live.

In contrast to the hopelessness of the Buddhist religious system, the Thai people like to enjoy themselves. One of the most important words in the Thai language is *sanuk*, "fun." So religious festivals and celebrations have become times for great revelry.

Probably the most enjoyable festival is *Songkran*, the Thai New Year, on April 13. The holiday was originally designed as a time to wash the Buddha statues and as a time of renewal. In towns and villages throughout the country, there are parades with musical instruments and dancing and a large Buddha statue carried through the village. Somewhere along the line the washing of the Buddha statues got a little out of hand, and people starting throwing water on each other. Since April is the hottest month of the year in Thailand, no one seemed to mind. Now *Songkran*, in addition to the washing of Buddha statues, is a giant, nationwide water-throwing celebration. For three days businesses close, and everyone throws water on each other. It is great fun.

Loy Krathong is a festival held in November each year in which people construct small boats made of banana leaves. In the middle of the boat they place a candle. In the evening the candles are lit and the boats are floated down the river, creating an impressive sight. *Loy Krathong* is an opportunity for the people to float their sins of the past year down the river with the banana leaf boat. In some places the boats are thought to be a way to appease the river spirits or ask forgiveness for polluting the rivers.

One of the most unusual festivals in Thailand is the Chinese Vegetarian Festival. The Chinese give up eating meat of any kind for several weeks (much like our Christian idea of Lent). There are parades and celebrations in the streets and in the Chinese

Buddhist temples. Many of the people invite spirits to come into them and place them into a trance. Then these spirit-possessed people perform acts such as walking on burning coals or piercing their cheeks with a large metal rod several feet in length. They hang baskets of flowers or vegetables on each end of the rod and parade through the streets, demonstrating that there is no blood and no pain.

All these celebrations, however, only mask the hopelessness of Thai life. No amount of water throwing or candle floating can really forgive their sins. Only God can redeem them from their plight; only the gospel has the power to transform their lives.

While many people present the gospel as a way to eternal life, the Buddhist, who is seeking to escape the eternal life of reincarnation, needs to hear that Christ can offer forgiveness. He or she needs to know that Christ can break the cycle of karma and "set [anyone] free from the law of sin and death" (Rom. 8:2). The Buddhist needs Christ as personal Savior. That is why the Church of the Nazarene has come to Thailand.

4
Getting Past the Gobbledygook

JEAN R. KNOX

GOBBLEDYGOOK! I knew I was in trouble the moment I stepped off the plane in Bangkok and heard sounds from Thai people that were unintelligible to my ears. How could God create such beautiful people, place them in an exotic culture—and give them a language hard enough to make any sanctified missionary give up and book the first flight home?

Such questions, I guess, are reserved for resolution in eternity. Like all first-term missionaries, my husband and I faced the tasks of language study and cultural adaptation. People who study such things have found that these tasks follow a predictable pattern of fascination, hostility and disenchantment, then resolution and adjustment.

After Richard and I were appointed to Thailand in 1988, one of my first responses was to find a copy of Thai script. I went to a library and located a page from a book in the Thai language. I was utterly enthralled by the beauty of Thai script. These unique, gracefully crafted, strange-looking letters danced across the page. I don't think I heard violins playing when my eyes first spied the language, but there was a certain holy awe in seeing the written language of "my people." I immediately began to pray and to covet being able to communicate in this new language, a task I knew to be vital to our success as missionaries. After all, I thought, how hard can a new language be?

เพราะว่าพระเจ้าทรงรักโลก จนได้ทรงประทานพระบุตรองค์เดียวของพระองค์
เพื่อทุกคนที่วางใจในพระบุตรนั้นจะไม่พินาศ แต่มีชีวิตนิรันดร์

(John 3:16 in the Thai Bible)

Then the plane landed. We had met all the educational requirements to become missionaries. We had survived all the difficult good-byes to our families at the airport. Now we had arrived on our field of service ready to see millions come to Christ in the first week. There was only one little problem: this language, which had looked so beautiful on the printed page, was unintelligible to us, and I could not understand what these people were saying!

Oh, well—I knew I would "get the language" in language school. After all, there were other things on my fascination list that encouraged me during those initial days: the kindness and courtesy of the Thai people; the gorgeous, extravagant-looking architecture of Thai Buddhist temples; modern skyscrapers and shopping malls (instead of the expected huts); and the new friendship and support of our coworkers, Mike and Rachel McCarty. I decided that this new country was livable and not bad at all!

I distinctly remember the morning I lost my fascination with the country. Early one Sunday morning I awoke and thought, "This has been a nice place to visit, but I want to go home." Questions started shooting through my brain: "Why did I choose to come here?" "Why did I fill out all those applications to become a missionary?" "How will I ever learn this frustrating language with 44 consonants, 24 vowels, 32 combinations, and 5 speaking tones with no spaces between the words and no punctuation?" It is a humbling experience to leave one's country with a master's degree and arrive in another country only to feel like a babbling idiot!

This realization was quickly followed by many others. Suddenly I noticed how filthy the streets were. The cockroaches were ever before me. Some odors on the street or in the market almost knocked me down. I got so tired of eating rice, rice, and more rice. I was overwhelmed with seeing Thai letters on billboards all over my new city. I daydreamed about buying gallons of paint and painting all the Thai billboards in English.

During this period of disenchantment, some of the cultural differences of Thai people at times overwhelmed me. They had so many different ways of doing things. In Thai culture one must cover one's mouth with a hand when using a toothpick. However, it is perfectly good manners to pick your nose in public.

Laughter in Thai culture doesn't necessarily mean that a situation is comical. It sometimes shows embarrassment, surprise, or serves as a stress release. For example, on one occasion our son was ill, so I took him to a Thai doctor. When the doctor performed a painful procedure, our son began to cry. As the procedure continued, the doctor and her nurses nervously laughed through the whole ordeal. They were not laughing at our child's pain. They were simply releasing their uncomfortable feelings resulting from treating a foreigner's child with that foreigner present in the room during the procedure. Laughter is the way some Thai people get through difficult situations.

Truth is hard to validate in Thai culture. People sometimes tell you what you want to hear rather than the absolute truth. It is important to word a question very carefully. For example, suppose a Thai person arrives unexpectedly at your house at dinnertime. If you invite the person to join your family for the dinner meal, he or she will probably refuse, saying that he or she has already eaten. However, this person might be referring to lunch so as not to inconvenience your family by joining your dinner meal.

Children are valued very highly in Thai culture. It is not uncommon to see Thais touching a child's head, face, or arm out in public. These gestures show their deep love for children and their desire to express that love in a tangible way. When we arrived on the field with our son, a cute six-year-old who wore glasses, people couldn't resist touching his white skin, since they find Caucasian children absolutely adorable. Thais also believe that people with white skin have the highest status in the world.

It took time to work through all of these new

cultural experiences. In spite of my lack of totally understanding the Thai people, God was in control even in those beginning days of figuring out the cultural puzzle of our new missionary situation.

Thankfully, all those days, weeks, and months of language school eventually paid off. God enabled me to adjust to a hot, tropical climate, traffic jams that cause an eight-mile errand to take two hours, and the lack of American punctuality. God also helped me realize that I will never be Thai and that my Thai friends will never be American, but that we can enjoy and celebrate His unique gifting of us through both cultural backgrounds and learn from each other.

The 18 months of language school was time well spent, but we were thankful for the chance to move on and develop our friendships with the Thai people. After all, Jesus did not come to die for a language, but for people. However, we could not have reached these people with the love of Christ without first taking the time to see the world through their eyes and articulate it in their language.

When I arrived in Thailand, I had to become a little child again, learning a whole new set of cultural and language rules for living. In this way God enables His missionaries to tell His message in a way that will be understood by His chosen people in every world area. He calls us, equips us, and sees us through these culture shock experiences. There is nothing too hard for Him!

By the miracle of God's grace I made the adjustment, and wonderful things began to happen. Suddenly I could understand that strange jargon Thais were speaking that used to be so frustrating. I could read the billboards in Thai. I could hold a conversation with a Thai speaker and comprehend most of what was said.

But I hadn't really arrived yet. In some ways missionaries never arrive. Language and culture learning are lifelong experiences. Those first 18 months of language school were an introduction to what will be a lifetime journey of learning. An important part of that learning process for people in ministry is learning to read and use God's Word.

When a missionary to Thailand leaves language school, he or she has usually taken a 20-day Bible course, because the Thai Bible is written in high language, not the ordinary street language of the Thai people. The high language is a specialized language used when referring to the royal family in Thailand. Since Thai Christians believe that God is higher than their national king, the Bible must be written in high language to show proper respect to God. That all sounds logical and admirable until you find yourself facing this lengthy text. High language uses specialized vocabulary and phrases not only in the Bible but also for prayer language.

All that makes it easy to make a mistake when praying or preaching. One missionary was starting his prayer, intending to say, "O great God," and mistakenly said, "O fat lady." Another missionary, preaching about Moses and the burning bush, quoted God as telling Moses to "fry his shoes" rather than to take them off.

What a challenge to remember special words, sentence structure, speaking tones, vocabulary, and content all at once! It is only through determination, perseverance, study, practice, prayer, and God's marvelous grace that we missionaries learn to use our Thai Bibles. Charles Gailey tells students at Nazarene Theological Seminary that when new missionaries get to the point that they weep over the language, they've almost gotten it. There are many tearstains in the Bibles of missionaries to Thailand.

Once I had become a culture shock survivor, it was time to get involved in ministry among my people. And God lovingly placed the right Thai and Lahu people in my path. If I had not put in all those months of study, I wouldn't be about to minister to those people, people like Siripawn Malagoon.

Siripawn was born in southern Thailand to a Buddhist family. After I completed language school, Siripawn came to me, desiring to study piano. She had no previous knowledge or experience in music, and her qualifications were a teachable spirit and a willingness to practice.

Through our association, Siripawn, the only Christian in her entire family, became a charter member of Bangkok First Church. Her desire to be involved in music ministry led her to be the pianist for worship services at the church. She is also taking ministerial training classes, and only God knows the plans He has for her life.

Looking at people like Siripawn and the hundreds of others like her whom I have met since those early days, I am continually reminded how important those early days of study have been. Without them, none of what I have done since would have been possible. The joy of the harvest is well worth any sacrifices necessary to plant the seeds.

5
Sowing and Reaping

W. RICHARD KNOX

When the Michael McCarty family (Michael, Rachel, and Deborah) and our family (Richard, Jean, Karissa, and William) arrived in Bangkok in 1989, we and a few contacts were all that the Church of the Nazarene had in Thailand. Our initial assignment and primary responsibility was to study the language for the first year and a half. While it was frustrating to change from having weekly ministry just prior to coming to Thailand to doing no other ministry except language study during this time, it was a wise decision on the part of the World Mission Division to emphasize language learning first. All our future ministry in Thailand would be built upon this foundation.

However, besides language study, we spent those first 18 months surveying the city, looking at new neighborhoods, and finding areas where churches were located. We needed to know which areas had no churches and what the population of those areas was like in order to plan our ministry effectively. It was tedious but important work.

We also spent time visiting many different Thai churches. We wanted to observe how Thais worship, what Thai leaders were like, and how they shared the gospel. In all this, plus occasional days of just sight-seeing, we attempted to gather as much information as we could about Thai culture and the Thai Christian community prior to planting the Church of the Nazarene in Bangkok.

During our language study we began Bible study groups in our homes. These were times of fellowship for us and some of our Thai friends, as well as much-needed opportunities to relax after a stressful week of language study. We prayed together for the beginning of the church in Thailand. We used these occasions to build close relationships with our team and adopt common goals for our future ministry.

In May 1990 we leased a facility in the Bangkapi area of Bangkok for 30 years. Bangkapi is located near Ramkhamhaeng University, which is reported to be the largest "open university" in the world, with an estimated 700,000 students enrolled, though only about 10 percent actually attend classes on campus. Our research had indicated that college-age young adults were the most receptive to the gospel of Jesus Christ. So our plan was to begin planting the church among young adults and then train them as workers and leaders to take the gospel to other parts of the city and country.

Our newly leased building was located near an area of rapid growth. New roads and businesses were under construction. New shopping centers and schools were in the plans. Thousands of housing units—apartments, condominiums, and homes—were either being built or were planned for the area. We believed this would be an ideal, growing area for the future of the church.

Our building in Bangkapi is a four-story shophouse, one of many commonly used throughout Asia for small businesses and offices. Inside, it was an empty concrete shell, so we had to completely remodel and furnish the interior. When we finished, it contained offices, kitchen, and reception area on the first floor, classrooms on the second floor, a sanctuary for the new church plant on the third floor, an apartment for church workers on the fourth floor, and a baptistery on the roof. General Superintendent Raymond W. Hurn dedicated our new building on January 11, 1991, during his official visit to Thailand. Prior to that, we began our first church services in October 1990, with 25 in attendance.

First service at Bangkok First Church

At first we had only our two families and two part-time Thai workers, Warnnachai Donchan and Somsak Naitip. A few months later Somsak Naitip became the first full-time pastor of Bangkok First Church. Charter members were received on Pentecost Sunday in 1991, and the church was organized with an elected church board in June of that year. General Superintendent John A. Knight officially organized the Thailand District on January 19, 1992, and the following October the Evangelical Fellowship of Thailand recognized the Church of the Nazarene as one of its members. The foundation for the future was being laid block by block.

In September 1992 Somsak Naitip returned to his home province in Chiang Rai, and Rev. Daniel Saengwichai became the pastor of Bangkok First Church. Daniel and his wife, Pachara, had helped the Church of the Nazarene with translation and radio work prior to joining the church. Through their ministry, the young church in the capital continued to grow and to reach out aggressively to the university students in the area. It was a special day for Bangkok First Church members when their pastor was ordained as our first Thai elder by General Superintendent Donald D. Owens at the third Thailand District Assembly in January 1994.

All this progress did not happen without much work and the use of many different evangelistic tools. One of our greatest assets was the ever present radio. World Mission Radio offerings provided for radio programs like *The Heart's Rest* on Saturday evening or *Good Morning, Bangkok!* on Sunday morning. Other avenues we used to invite non-

Christians to come to the church were English and piano classes. Our Christians would make friends with the non-Christians who came to study and then invite them to come to the church services.

Since fun and celebration are important aspects of Thai culture (the Thai word for "work" is used in the phrase "to have a party"), we used special days for celebrations in the church. On our first Christmas in the Bangkapi building, we had over 100 people come to a Christmas dinner and program. Now not only Christmas but also Valentine's Day, Mother's Day, and other special holidays have become part of our celebration times. We invite non-Christians to these celebrations, where the gospel is presented.

Another "fun" avenue of ministry is our soccer program. Participants come for the fun of playing ball, but they are also exposed to the gospel, to Christian people, and to the church.

By far the most important evangelistic tools we have are our personal relationships. While that is true in the United States, it is even more true in Asia. Most of the visitors to church, and most of the new converts, have come because of their friendship with a Christian. As the church members became excited about what was happening at their church, they invited their friends. Non-Christians are accepted and loved into the fellowship. We have even conducted personal evangelism classes and cell groups to make these relationships even more fruitful.

We have seen the benefits of these relationships firsthand at Bangkok First Church. As I mentioned, the church is located near Ramkhamhaeng University. Guy was a young student at the university when she found Christ through our radio ministry. When she accepted the Lord, she began to use her relationships with other students at Ramkhamhaeng University to introduce them to Him. Guy introduced Phitsamai to the church. Phitsamai invited Bootsabong. Someone in their group invited Weerarat. All these young ladies come from non-Christian homes. Today all have accepted Christ and have joined the Church of the Nazarene. These young ladies are now serving in positions of leadership in Bangkok First Church as church board members and Nazarene Youth International (NYI) officers.

And the webs of influence and circles of relationships continue to multiply. Guy also invited a young lady nicknamed "Ang" to church. Ang was a new student at Ramkhamhaeng University and had never been away from home. She was very shy at first, but she began to blossom when she found acceptance at the Church of the Nazarene. We pray that soon Ang will also make the decision to accept Christ as her Savior.

Thong was raised in a Christian home and was looking for a church near the university when he was introduced to the Church of the Nazarene. He invited his brother and sister to church too. All three are now actively involved in the church. His sister, Yupa, serves as the local church treasurer and as the district treasurer. As the web continues to grow, so does Bangkok First Church.

In the city of Surin, located in northeastern

Thailand, the Khmer connection (see next chapter) and the resulting relationships became the impetus for a new church. Through contacts and relationships with Cambodian refugees there, a group of Thai believers began to worship together under the leadership of Suphannaret Duangwimol, a Cambodian who can speak both Khmer and Thai. He provided the natural link between the two language groups as our work began in Surin.

As the time for repatriation of the Cambodians drew near, we anticipated Suphannaret's return to his homeland. Suphannaret introduced us to Ded Thiapthong, who became the pastor of our Thai church in Surin. The church began to meet in the home of Pastor Ded and was officially organized in January 1993. Through the combined efforts of Alabaster giving and a Korean Work and Witness team, a new building for our Surin church was dedicated in January 1995.

In July 1994, Prasan Thongsumat and his family became a part of the Church of the Nazarene, and he began planting a new church in the northeastern city of Maha Sarakham. With the support of the district, a building near the bus station was rented to begin services. Prasan was soon leading a group of new believers through Chic Shaver's *Basic Bible Studies*. Membership classes followed in anticipation that the young Maha Sarakham church would soon be fully organized. Recently the congregation moved to a new location, and has begun to look for land for a permanent church building.

Prior to joining the Church of the Nazarene, missionary Samuel Yangmi worked as an independent missionary among the Lahu tribes in northern Thailand (see chaps. 1 and 7). The churches that Sam had established expressed their desire to follow Sam and join the Church of the Nazarene. In the early months of 1994, Mike McCarty and Sam Yangmi traveled to each mountain village to teach membership classes and to receive new members. New Nazarene churches were organized in Huay Tad, Nong Wua Daeng, Pa Sak, and Huay Luang. Later in the year the church in Pa Yang was also organized.

And so the Thailand District has grown. Through many different methods, many different people, and connections from many different countries, God has been at work building His Church. Sometimes church planting has been more a matter of providence than a matter of planning. Sometimes we missionaries have felt as though we were playing catch-up in responding to the opportunities the Lord has given us. Sometimes our church planting plans have worked well, while at other times they have failed. Yet through it all God has been at work building His Church.

And that, after all, is the main point: it is Christ's Church. And He promised that He would build His Church. What a privilege it is to be a part of His Church-building team! We are always amazed at what He is doing in and through His Church here. Though problems arise, though difficulties come, though sometimes we do not even know what to do next, we continue on in the confidence that God is faithful and will indeed establish His kingdom in the kingdom of Thailand.

6

The Khmer Connection

MICHAEL P. MCCARTY

ON APRIL 17, 1975, the Cambodian capital of Phnom Penh fell to the Khmer Rouge. In the four years that followed, terror, disease, starvation, and death swept over Thailand's eastern neighbor. Between 1 and 3 million Cambodians died. Tens of thousands were tortured, killed, and thrown into unmarked graves at one of the many "killing fields" throughout the country. The Khmer people who were outside of Cambodia and those inside who could escape began an exodus to the West. The majority fled to France, Australia, or the United States.

When the army of Vietnam defeated the Khmer Rouge and retook the Cambodian capital on January 7, 1979, the exodus of people intensified. This time, however, people fled through minefields to the border of northeastern Thailand. Thousands died or were maimed in the attempt.

Although at first resisted by the Thai military, the flood of Cambodian refugees could not be stopped. The United Nations finally stepped in to create order, security, and operational structure in the various refugee camps established along the Thai-Cambodian border. At the peak of their exile, an estimated 390,000 Khmer refugees lived inside Thailand.

While living in the camps, the refugees in Thailand contacted family members who had fled to the United States and other nations. A system of communication was soon established that enabled relatives to send money and personal items to the refugees. Since the Church of the Nazarene had established several Cambodian churches in the early 1980s among those who had fled to America, news soon sped back to Thailand about a church that cared about the Khmer people in exile. More and more refugees who made it to the United States were being incorporated into Cambodian Nazarene churches.

In 1988 the gospel was presented via mail to some Khmer refugees living in the Site B Camp near the city of Surin in northeastern Thailand. After several letters had crossed the Pacific Ocean, an invitation was extended to the Nazarenes to come over and help. Soon the New Life Cambodian Church of the Nazarene (and her parent body, Long Beach, California, First Church) was making plans to visit these refugees and explore possibilities of future church planting both in Thailand and also within the nation of Cambodia once peace was restored.

In December 1988, George Rench (Asia-Pacific regional director), Brent Cobb (Long Beach First Church mission director), Ratlief Ung (New Life Cambodian Church pastor), and others arrived in Thailand to visit the refugees in Site B Camp and the group working at the Khmer printshop in the city of Surin. The gospel was presented again in greater clarity, and plans were made for a follow-up visit by the Nazarene missionaries who were soon to arrive in Thailand.

In August 1989 Dr. Rench was back in Thailand. Together with missionaries Mike McCarty and Richard Knox, the promised follow-up visit was made. By 1990, monthly drives from Bangkok to Surin were the routine for the latter two men. From June 1990 until June 1991, over 55 new Khmer believers were baptized into the Christian faith. Church membership classes were started, and the Surin (Khmer) Church of the Nazarene was officially organized in June 1991. One of the charter members of this church was Ven Runnath.

Mrs. Ven Runnath

As a young girl growing up in central Cambodia, Mrs. Ven and her classmates had been trained in the Buddhist religion. During her days of religious education in the temple, Mrs. Ven was taught the Buddhist doctrines of suffering, karma, and reincarnation, as well as the prophecy about "the Buddha who is to come." She learned that when this new Buddha comes, the world would be changed to a place of peace, beauty, and happiness.

Since there were so many religious teachers in the world, Mrs. Ven asked how one would know this Buddha when he came. She was told that he would have five marks on his body—one on his head, one on each hand, and one on each foot. As a young girl amazed at what she had learned, she wanted so much to meet this Buddha when he came.

Mrs. Ven married a pilot and was working at a bank in Phnom Penh when the Khmer Rouge took over the capital. Since her husband held the rank of lieutenant colonel in the air force, he was killed immediately. Mrs. Ven took her husband's name—Runnath—and fled with the rest of the family into the countryside.

During the next four years Mrs. Ven suffered much. The families of the military were hunted down and eliminated to avoid any retribution for the Khmer Rouge leaders in the future. Mrs. Ven lost children to both disease and starvation during these four years. If she had not lapsed into a temporary case of insanity and then into a coma under the stress of it all, she would have been killed. As it was, she was just left to die. Somehow she lived and remembers hearing her mother calling her name to come back to them and help with the care of the children.

Soon afterward the news arrived that the Khmer Rouge had been defeated by the Vietnamese. Taking her mother and her remaining children—two sons and a daughter—Mrs. Ven began the trek across the minefields to the Thai border. They walked and hid for days, eating what little food they could find in the jungle. Then one day they arrived at one of the refugee camps near Surin.

While in the camp, Mrs. Ven was introduced to Christianity by social workers who shared the love of Christ with her. Seeing a picture of Christ hanging on the Cross, with the nails in His hands and feet and the blood streaming down from His head from the crown of thorns, Mrs. Ven remembered the prophecy about the Buddha who would come to bring peace and happiness to the world. Convinced that this Buddha had already come in the person of Jesus Christ, she accepted Jesus as her Savior and became a faithful disciple.

When the Church of the Nazarene arrived at Site B, Mrs. Ven and her family were permitted to move out of the camp and live in the nearby town of Prasat, halfway between Site B Camp and the city of Surin. She met Nancy Clark, who was a minister with the Nazarene Cambodian work in Minnesota and therefore knew quite a bit about the Church of the Nazarene. Mrs. Ven helped us disciple the new believers coming to Christ. Since she spoke four languages—English, French, Thai, and Khmer—she served both as interpreter for our worship services and as translator for our church membership material.

There at Site B the ministry of the Church of the Nazarene extended beyond the conducting of worship services. Nazarene Compassionate Ministries helped make life more bearable in the dry, dust-filled camp. Along with a young Khmer lady named Oum Sophea, the director of an orphanage in Site B, the church also sponsored a program to help children prepare for returning to their country.

The United Nations wanted to ensure that the Khmer Cambodians were returned to their country in time for the May 1992 elections. To that end the church sponsored a mobile community center to teach children about life outside the camp. Most of the children aged 10 years and younger had never known anything else but life in the dusty, crowded refugee camp. We hoped that this project would help prepare them for their eventual transition to a normal life.

In cooperation with the camp authorities, Site B was divided into 27 sections, with each section containing approximately 100 to 200 children. Each day a specially constructed cart was pushed to a new section (making the rounds to each section once a month), and the equipment was set up for a two-hour community program by the trained staff.

The children often sat crowded wall to wall as they were taught basic health education, played group games, learned about the world outside the camp, and were given some treats at the end. Their voices rang out in unison as they repeated their lessons by rote. The funds were limited, and often there were not enough materials to go around, but this approach served the children well for two years until it was discontinued at the beginning of the repatriation process. Interestingly enough, Prince Sirivudh, the official with whom we worked closely on this project, was later to become the Cambodian foreign minister.

Children at the Site B Camp

In the centuries of struggle over who would control Southeast Asia, northeastern Thailand was once a part of Cambodia, and at another time northwestern Cambodia was once a part of Thailand. As a result, many of the Thai citizens in and around the city of Surin are ethnic Khmer. They can speak Khmer but cannot read and write that language.

Thus, as work was progressing with the Khmer refugees and our Cambodian Nazarene church in Surin, news about our church was also being spread to the Thai citizens in the area. Eventually, contact was made with a core group of these citizens who desired to become a part of our Nazarene family. This dual-language group eventually formed the nucleus of our Thai-speaking Church of the Nazarene in Surin, becoming an officially organized church in January 1992. Later a Khmer songbook was compiled, in which the Khmer language was written in the Thai script so that Thai Christians could sing the Khmer songs.

Our first missionaries to the nation of Cambodia, Rev. and Mrs. Ratlief Ung, left the pastorate of New Life Cambodian Church in Long Beach and arrived in Phnom Penh in April 1992. Although the Khmer church in Surin has now been officially disorganized in Thailand, through it the gospel has been carried back to Cambodia. The Good News and the Church of the Nazarene continue to bear fruit in Cambodia even to this day with some of our former members from Surin becoming a part of Phnom Penh First Church.

In April 1993, Rev. and Mrs. Hae-Rim (Philip) Park were appointed as missionaries to Southeast Asia as the first regional missionaries of the Asia-Pacific Region. Fully supported by the Korean National Board, the Parks were appointed for an initial two-year term. They were the vanguard of what George Rench had envisioned as the coming of age of the Asian church—not only receiving missionaries but also now being able to equip, fund, and send them out.

The Parks were first assigned to Cambodia.

However, due in part to the uneasy political situation at that time and the fear and uncertainty of what the Khmer Rouge might do just prior to the national elections, the decision was made to reassign them to Thailand. After language study, they moved to Surin in August 1994 to assist the local church, provide additional training for their pastor, and to supervise the construction of the new church building.

As the congregation in Surin grew, land was purchased with Alabaster funds for a future building. Soon the Korea Central District funded a building project. A Work and Witness team from Korea arrived in November 1994 to begin the project, and a two-story building was dedicated on January 26, 1995. Representatives from the Korea Central District were present for the occasion. This church building stands today as a witness to the efforts of local, district, and national leaders from three countries.

From Cambodia to Thailand and back again, from Seoul to Surin and from Bangkok to Site B, the interconnectedness and partnership of our international Nazarene family in the cause of global mission continues to grow. While we rejoice in what has been accomplished so far, we are praying for the day when the mines along the Thailand-Cambodia border are removed, and those at war lay down their weapons in peace. We look forward to the day when the ethnic Khmer, Thai Christians will be able to walk across the border to speak the good news of Jesus to their Cambodian neighbors. Someday it will happen. And we want to be prepared when it does.

7
The Golden Triangle

ERIC KELLERER, SAMUEL YANGMI, AND BRENT COBB

THE RAIN HAD BEEN FALLING for days. Forty-three years had passed since Thailand had experienced such a heavy rainy season, and this one would not soon be forgotten. Four dams had burst, destroying farmland and homes. Many people were being flooded from their homes. Even so, when the invitation came for the Church of the Nazarene to visit three Red Lahu villages, it was impossible to refuse. These villages, located high in the mountains of northern Thailand in an area known as the Golden Triangle, had been completely unreceptive to any approach by Christians in the past, but God was answering prayer.

It was agreed that Sam Yangmi, Eric Kellerer, and three Lahu men would make the trip. The truck was loaded with supplies, and we were on our way. After three uneventful hours on paved roads, we parked the truck at the entrance to a dirt road. Many people were gathered there, selling and trading, and they immediately came to look us over. After the usual casual greetings, we asked, "Can we make it to Sheh Taw village?" With few exceptions, the people said it would be impossible.

Knowing that God wanted His Word preached to these villages, we decided to attempt to reach them. Locking the hubs of the four-wheel-drive truck was the first and easiest thing that we would do for the rest of that day. We managed to get a full 75 yards down the dirt road before we had to put the mud chains on all four wheels. Twenty minutes later we were under way. However, after another 50 yards we were digging ourselves out of the mud.

Four hours later we had gone a total of 3 miles, and we had about 12 miles to go. It started to rain again, so we decided to turn back, but we had not yet given up.

The next morning we were up early, ate a good hot and spicy breakfast, and drove to the river. There is something both majestic and terrifying about a river at flood stage. At times it looked like a muddy, peaceful river, but parts of homes and floating trees were testimonies to the crushing power of the water upstream.

However, the flood didn't seem to bother the boat driver. In no time we had loaded the long-tail boat with our supplies and crowded in for the trip upstream. Somehow we sensed that there was a supernatural Copilot in our boat that day. In spite of the destruction that we pushed through for the next two hours, we all knew that God was leading us and that this was His chosen time for these three villages to hear His Word.

We stepped off the boat, not knowing what to

expect. The next 24 hours were filled with sipping tea, sharing stories, and slopping through the mud from one village to the next.

The highlight of the trip was sitting together in the light of the fire talking with the headman of Ti Sheh village. After much storytelling, laughter, and illustrations, he looked at Sam Yangmi and said, "I want you to know you are welcome here, not just as a visitor, but as my son who has been gone for a long time and has now returned. While you are here in our village, you will be called 'Ca Naw Kha,' the Golden Awakener." In the few short hours we had in these villages, the leaders of the villages realized that the truth for which they had been searching was contained in the Word of God.

Samuel Yangmi with his wife, Lumae, and four daughters Anzie, Samantha, Julie, Nellie.

The next day we slid through the mud down the mountain and back to the waiting boat. We knew we would come back to these villages. We knew there was a lot of work to be done, but we also knew we had witnessed the beginning of something great the Lord had done.

It would be inappropriate to leave the reader of this chapter with the impression that this event just happened on its own without any prior contact, prayers, or groundwork. What we witnessed in those three villages is the result of years of seed planting and nurture. It is the result of God's incredible orchestration of events in the lives of individuals, as well as the leadership of the Church of the Nazarene. As is so often the case, God began to plant a seed in Thailand long before our arrival. Many years before the Church of the Nazarene was officially registered in Thailand, God had already chosen one of the missionaries who would play a key role here.

Samuel Yangmi was born in southern China to Chinese Lisu parents who were fleeing the Communists in China in 1955. Knowing the danger they faced, his parents gave him up for adoption to a young lady named Esther Morse, daughter of missionaries Russell and Gertrude Morse. Esther later married a young man named Jesse Yangmi.

Ten years later the Communists controlled Burma, and the Yangmis and Morses were forced, along with thousands of other Christians, from the country. Denied permission to enter India, they settled in an unadministered border area that came to be known as Hidden Valley.* More than 20 Christian villages were established there until they were forced to leave again six years later.

In 1970 the Yangmis left Hidden Valley for the United States so Jesse could continue his education. So it was that young Samuel attended high school in Joplin, Missouri. In 1975 Jesse and Esther Yangmi went to northern Thailand. A year later Sam joined them there to help with a revision of the Lisu Bible and do village evangelism.

During his first term in Thailand, Sam did independent missionary work among the Lisu hilltribe people living near the Thailand-Burma border. He also went from village to village evangelizing among the non-Christians and learning a new language, Lahu. In 1978 Sam married a Lahu girl named Lumae. Their work as missionaries continued with the Lisu people but increasingly took root among the Lahu people as well.

The Lahu people are seminomadic tribesmen, having no claim to any part of Thailand as their home. They have their own culture and language and are quite different from their Thai neighbors. The Lahu are at least half a million strong and spread through five countries (Myanmar, China, Laos, Vietnam, and Thailand), numbering about 60,000 in 150 villages in Thailand itself.

The Lahu people believe in many good, bad, and neutral spirits. They do, however, believe in a Supreme Spirit that is above all others. The non-

---

*For more information, see Eugene Morse, *Exodus to Hidden Valley* (New York: Reader's Digest Press, 1974).

Christian Lahu does not know who this Supreme Being is or how to know Him personally. Sam worked to introduce the Lahu man or woman to the Supreme Being, namely God, through His Son Jesus Christ. Many Lahu came to know Christ and were freed from having to appease the evil spirits through animal sacrifices and the burning of incense because they knew Christ as their Protector and their Lord.

Working with the Lahu made Sam realize the need to have more development work, especially through the education of tribal children and agricultural projects to replace opium crops, upon which the livelihood of many of the Lahu people depended. So the Yangmis returned to the United States on furlough, and through God's direction they found a school in which Sam could study not only theology but also agriculture. That school was MidAmerica Nazarene College in Olathe, Kansas.

In 1984, when Sam and Lumae left MidAmerica Nazarene College, they returned to Thailand with more than a degree. They returned with a love and appreciation for the Church of the Nazarene. For two terms God continued to bless their work as independent missionaries. Their work in agriculture and evangelism escalated with the planting of new churches in four Lahu villages and the establishment of the Maetang Tribal Children's Home.

Most of the remote hill-tribe villages do not have schools. The Maetang Tribal Children's Home provides an opportunity for children to attend a public school while living in a secure Christian environment. While at the home, the children also receive instruction in the Bible and work skills in agriculture and in raising animals. (Presently, approximately half of the 200 or so children have received sponsorship through the Child Sponsorship Program of Nazarene Compassionate Ministries.)

Having helped the Church of the Nazarene enter Thailand, the Yangmis decided to form an even closer attachment with the denomination. During their 1993 furlough, the Yangmis joined College Church of the Nazarene in Olathe, Kansas, and returned to Thailand as Nazarene missionaries to continue the tribal work. In 1994 the independent Lahu churches that the Yangmis had been working with for many years merged with the Church of the Nazarene, thus tripling the membership of the young Thailand District.

Throughout the Yangmis' time among the Lahu people, they have spent many hours developing a relationship of trust and confidence within the villages. As people move from one village to the next, and as children return to their villages after living in the Maetang Tribal Children's Home, the gospel continues to spread among the Lahu people.

As this book is being written, we are looking forward to reaching more non-Christian villages like the three Red Lahu villages mentioned at the beginning of the chapter. There will be several opportunities for Work and Witness teams to be involved in building churches and a new dormitory at the Maetang Tribal Children's Home. A pastoral training center is in the planning stages to train men and women for leadership. We want to give them a strong biblical and practical education while still allowing them to be involved in their areas of ministry.

Of course, the work in the Golden Triangle is not limited solely to the Lahu or other tribal groups. There are many ethnic Thai people who need to hear the gospel as well. The challenge will be much like that in Bangkok and other areas of Thailand: to reach out to a strongly Buddhist people and help them see the need for Jesus Christ. We look forward to starting churches among as many people as possible.

The Golden Triangle represents a field that is white unto harvest with few workers. The challenge is a great one. We are thankful for God's Word in Rev. 7:9, which describes "a great multitude that no one could count, from every nation, tribe, people and language, standing before the throne and in front of the Lamb." We missionaries rejoice that the Lahu people as well as other tribal groups will be among that throng of people in heaven!

8

What Do All Those Letters Mean?

ERIC KELLERER, PAULA KELLERER, AND JEAN R. KNOX

WHAT DOES A THAI NAZARENE college student have in common with Nazarene college students in Africa, Europe, or America? The answer may surprise you. Imagine a young Thai who has graduated from college in Thailand. He has had years of English courses when he leaves Thailand to travel abroad to further his education. Imagine his delight when he gets to his first overseas Nazarene church service and sits down to read the bulletin:

> The NWMS will be sponsoring a reception to honor the recently returning W&W team, as well as the Smiths, who were NIVS in the MAC Region. We will meet in the NYI hall right after the SS Board adjourns their meeting on sponsoring a YIM team.

The exciting thing about most of these acronyms is that a young Thai who is active in the Church of the Nazarene in Thailand will know what many of these letters mean from firsthand experience. In fact, he understands that these letters represent people. They represent brothers and sisters in Christ, new friends. For the remainder of this chapter we want to consider the impact volunteers have had on the growth of the kingdom of God here in Thailand, especially that of Youth in Mission (YIM), Nazarenes in Volunteer Service (NIVS), and Work and Witness (W&W).

Each year hundreds of Nazarenes from around the world volunteer their time to be a part of the mission of the church on the mission field. Many times the true benefits of these volunteers are not realized until they have long since returned home to their jobs and their friends. A great example of this was the 1994 Youth in Mission team to Thailand.

In Bangkok the team, three young adults working with Eric and Paula Kellerer, primarily worked on the campus of Ramkhamhaeng University. Ramkhamhaeng University is a massive campus, and presenting the gospel there was a unique challenge. There are 700,000 students associated with the university. Many of them come from remote areas of the country and will one day return to their villages. We pray that they will return carrying the gospel with them.

Outside of Bangkok the team was kept very busy doing Sunshine Clubs, special programs filled with puppets, music, and Scripture. Though the programs are designed for kids, adults love them too. It is difficult to describe the faces of the villagers when they see the puppets' heads pop over the stage for the first time. Most of them have never seen anything like it.

In Huay Luang, a Lahu village in northern Thailand, there were about 300 people crowded into a little building to witness the event. While the team was packing to leave after two days in the village, the oldest man in the village approached them. "I have had many good experiences in my life," he said, "but I have never, in all my life, laughed as hard as I have in these last two days. Thank you for bringing the meat of the gospel to our children and showing them that being a Christian can be fun too."

In July 1994 the YIM team spent three days in the village of Pa Yang. At that time the church was not yet organized, but it already had nine members. As we did not know what to expect, you can imagine our excitement as the pastor knocked out the back wall of the little bamboo church to make room for the almost 100 people who wanted to see the presentation.

While in the village, the team stopped to visit and pray with a little lady addicted to opium, but they also prayed that God would send revival among the people. Just two months after the YIM team was in the village of Pa Yang, 26 people wanted to be baptized. One month later, 35 people became charter members as the Pa Yang Church of the Nazarene was organized.

And the Youth in Mission concept continues to grow in Thailand. Today the Thai young people are not content to simply receive the blessings of those who volunteer. In the summer of 1996 the first Thai YIM team traveled to Korea to help with the Nazarene work there. So YIM has become an opportunity both to receive and to give a blessing in Thailand.

The Thailand field has also been enriched by the additional ministry of Nazarenes in Volunteer Service. The first person involved in NIVS ministry in Thailand was Janet Harman. In August 1989 Janet, a professor of education at Northwest Nazarene College in Nampa, Idaho, took a nine-month sabbatical to come to Thailand and teach Nazarene MKs (missionary kids). During her stay in Thailand, she taught sixth grade in a missionary children's cooperative school to enable missionaries Rachel McCarty and Jean Knox to attend Thai language school.

Janet describes her teaching experience in Thailand in this way:

> I loved my time in Thailand! I came back to the United States feeling that everyone should have such an experience. I loved the exposure to another culture. The time in Thailand planted an interest and a love for Asians in my heart. Without the exposure in Thailand, I don't think I would have ever reached out. Today, I have several lasting friendships with Chinese students from mainland China and have been able to play a part in sharing God's love with them. (In fact, I have a Chinese goddaughter!) I am also a volunteer ESL tutor for a Laotian man—and I would work with more students if I had the time.
>
> As for the MKs, I feel I had the most special group of students in the school! Although young in years, each of those sixth graders had a sense that they, too, were part of the missionary team their parents represented. It was a privilege to be

part of their lives for nine months—to view from the inside some of the special challenges they faced, yet also to see how they embraced their lifestyle in Thailand with contentment and enthusiasm.

Firsthand experience always provides more vivid insights than books and stories, and I think I came away from Thailand with a pretty realistic feel for the kinds of adjustments, challenges, annoyances, and problems encountered by missionaries. I think this experience has made me more sensitive to prayer requests on the behalf of missionaries, for I understand more about the implications involved.

Thailand's most recent NIVS personnel are Stephen and Linda Thomas, who arrived on the field in November 1995. Stephen had worked in Thailand 30 years ago as an English teacher at a university in southern Thailand. For the past 25 years he has been involved in ministry among refugees and has served as a church planter in multiethnic congregations in the United States.

The first six months after the Thomases arrived in Thailand were difficult ones. They lost a baby. They also had visa difficulties. Yet their testimony during this time was one of faithfulness to a loving God. Stephen said, "We could have just packed and gone home. But when God calls, we listen! The evil one could not and will not destroy our goal to serve in God's kingdom work in Thailand."

The Thomases are currently assisting Nazarene churches in Surin and Maha Sarakham in northeast Thailand. The Surin church is meeting in a new church building built on land purchased with Alabaster funds. Our new church plant in Maha Sarakham is already a healthy, growing congregation in one of the fastest-growing cities in northeast Thailand.

The Thomases' dream, however, is to return to Hat Yai, in southern Thailand, where Stephen taught English classes with the Peace Corps 30 years ago before he came to know the Lord. It is the Thomases' desire to tell the university students and professors there that Jesus is Lord and that He can make a difference in their lives.

If a shorter, hands-on ministry is what you are looking for, Work and Witness is the answer to your dreams. The first W&W team to Thailand arrived in September 1994 and were prepared for hands-on ministry. These five men from the Intermountain District faced personal and financial difficulties and overcame them through God's faithfulness.

They also faced a record-breaking monsoon season that washed away roads, flooded homes, and left northern Thailand in a muddy mess. Two weeks before the team arrived, all roads to the village of Huay Tad, where they planned to work, were closed. Parts of the road simply did not exist, having been washed down the mountainside. With God's help and a few brave men, the materials needed for their work were transported up the mountain to the village only hours before the team landed in Thailand.

The W&W team spent long days working with mortar, concrete, and cement blocks. The evenings and weekends were filled with preaching, teaching, and the sharing of testimonies. One Wednesday the team had been working hard, and many villagers were there throughout the day helping. By 5:30 P.M. they had poured an important section of concrete.

The team rushed down the hill for dinner in the home of the family with whom they were staying. After dinner came the weekly prayer meeting, which ended at 8 P.M. Not wanting to waste an opportunity, the villagers decided to pour more concrete. The next section was completed at about 10:30 P.M. This reveals the dedication of both W&W team members and villagers alike to accomplish what God had sent them to do.

The truly wonderful thing about that W&W team is that, not only did they bring their love, talents, and funds to encourage the Lahu people of Huay Tad, but also they took back with them the faces of real people who were touched through God's mission. They also took back the prayers of the people here. Two months after the team left Huay Tad, the church building was dedicated. Nearly 600 people came to celebrate Thanksgiving in the new structure.

Work and Witness is not limited to teams from North America. God sent a team of 16 Korean Nazarenes to help build the new church building in Surin. Again, this energetic team showed that W&W was more than raising a building. They helped the people of Thailand in many ways.

They brought eyeglasses to help church members who because of poor vision could no longer read the Bible. They distributed 20 bags of clothing among the needy. They gave an electronic keyboard to our evangelism team in the north. And those are

Korean Work and Witness team in Surin

not all the gifts that were carried in love from the country of Korea. Beyond the gifts came a commitment to pray for the needs and the people of Thailand and the commitment to encourage other Korean churches to become involved in W&W.

All over the country of Thailand plans were being prepared to bring the resources of God's people together for His glory. Work and Witness has a great future in this land. As the reader has seen in other chapters of this book, there are fields that are ripe for the harvest. We believe that the prayers of God's people are being answered as we move into new areas with the gospel. Work and Witness, NIVS personnel, and YIM teams will be a significant part of the future ministry plans in Thailand.

9
The Church on the Move

W. RICHARD KNOX AND MICHAEL P. MCCARTY

THE FIRST NAZARENE MISSIONARIES arrived in Thailand in 1989. Seven years have elapsed between the beginning days of those first language lessons and the time in which this book was written. At our fifth district assembly, held in Chiang Mai on January 22, 1996, the young Thailand District reported nine organized churches and seven new church plants. We had 404 full members and 64 associate ones, but we had an average worship attendance of 601, with 353 in Sunday School.

While we praise God for what has happened in a relatively short period, we need to now ask the questions "Where do we go from here?" and "How do we get there?" We cannot just rejoice in the past while the future for the millions in Thailand lies before us. The task of taking the gospel to the many around us will require the anointing and the direction of the Spirit, the dedication and the varied talents of the missionaries, the commitment and the personal ministry of the national church, and the prayers and support of the international family.

Our goal in Thailand is to be the catalyst in planting churches and districts that are self-governing, self-propagating, and self-supporting. We also aim to be "advancing the kingdom of God" as we "preserve and propagate Christian holiness as set forth in the Scriptures."* Thus the Church of the Nazarene around the world is committed to Holiness evangelism that will result in mature churches and districts that will impact their various nations for Christ. We hope to do this through many different means.

The first Church of the Nazarene in Thailand was planted by the missionaries in the city of Bangkok. However, if missionaries had to plant and pastor all of the churches, it would take the church in Thailand a long time to grow and even longer to properly mature. So after we started our first church, we needed to find a way to plant churches in other areas, a way not completely dependent upon the missionaries. We decided upon a "mission team" approach.

Using the mission team approach, a missionary or experienced Thai leader is paired with a Thai worker to plant a church in an area where there is no Nazarene church. These teams are sponsored by the mission or the district until the work grows to a point at which it can support itself. We are using this method to plant churches in all the major dis-

---

**Manual, Church of the Nazarene, 1993-97* (Kansas City: Nazarene Publishing House, 1993), 5.

tricts of Bangkok as well as Chiang Mai and the northeastern regional center of Khon Kaen.

Once a church grows large enough to begin other churches, such as Bangkok First Church has done, we use the strength of that mother church to start new satellite churches. We start cell groups, prayer groups, and Bible study groups in homes throughout the city. These groups help the local church to grow through the active involvement of our church members while at the same time providing outreach groups with the potential of organizing a new church. This model also helps develop strong lay leadership in the church.

One of the most effective methods of evangelism and church planting among the Lahu hill-tribe churches in northern Thailand is the sending of local evangelists to non-Christian villages. As the churches are burdened for their non-Christian neighbors, the local church arranges to send one of their own to share the good news of the gospel of Jesus Christ. Sometimes the district partners with them for establishing a church in a strategic village; sometimes the local church just decides to establish a church in the village on the next mountaintop. God is blessing not only their efforts of outreach but also their local churches who are supporting these evangelistic efforts.

Another important means of evangelism for the hill-tribe areas, and indeed all of Thailand, is family or personal evangelism. People are won to Christ through relationships with Christians they know. In the case of the hill tribes, one's family relationship is very important. If a relative living in one village visits a relative in another village and tells him or her about a personal relationship with Christ, the story is made more credible because of the family relationship. Entire villages have opened to the gospel because the evangelist was found to be a member in the family tree.

The churches we have in Isan, or northeastern Thailand, have experienced growth through youth work. Activities for children and teens have attracted young people and their families to the Church of the Nazarene. Recently several young people, who had never traveled beyond their home province, had the opportunity to go to the first Thailand District Youth Camp. Some of them found Jesus Christ as their Savior at camp. All returned home excited about their church.

Since two-thirds of the population of Isan, as well as the whole of Thailand, is under 30 years of age, the emphasis on youth work in this region of the nation is proving to be an effective strategy for reaching persons for Christ. The young people are more open to the gospel of Jesus Christ and are more responsive to the changes that Christ can make in their lives.

Planting all those churches makes sense only if one is going to equip ministers to serve in them, so we have begun ministerial training to prepare both pastors and evangelists for ordination. We teach intensive one-week courses and Saturday seminars in Bangkok, Chiang Mai, and Surin in order to prepare men and women for ordination within four or five years.

We have been overwhelmed by the response to

these classes, and it seems that many of our people are hungry for theological education. We hope to establish someday soon a Southeast Asia Nazarene Bible College. Based in Bangkok, this college would facilitate ministerial training by extension, not only in Thailand but also in Myanmar (Burma), Cambodia, Vietnam, and Laos.

As the church in Thailand moves toward being a self-governing, self-supporting church, we are moving to turn over leadership in the district to the emerging national leaders. Currently we have a District Advisory Board composed mainly of Thai leaders and a Thai district treasurer. We hope to have a Thai district superintendent by 1999.

But we hope that district development does not stop there. Our rapidly growing Lahu churches in the North could form their own district in just a few years. This would give those churches a greater sense of ownership in the work there as well as enable them to work more closely with their district superintendent. Presently the northern churches are 12 hours away from Bangkok. As both the northeast and the south of Thailand develop, we will organize new districts there as well.

As these districts develop, the support ministries of Sunday School, Nazarene Youth International, and the Nazarene World Mission Society become more and more important. Although many in Asia look upon the Sunday School as what the church does for children while the adults attend worship, the concept of Sunday School for all ages has been developing. Our churches need adequate curriculum and qualified teachers to make their

Sunday Schools work, and we have a Sunday School Committee working to address these needs.

The Nazarene Youth International program has been active on the district, due in part to the large number of youth in the Thai population. Our first District NYI Camp was held in April 1995 with 85 in attendance. We have a District NYI Council made up of a Thai president and six representatives, two from each main area of our district. This council is seeking to improve our church's ministry to youth throughout Thailand.

The Nazarene World Mission Society is the newest of the support ministries in Thailand. While the mission of the NWMS has been understood and actively practiced in Bangkok First Church since 1994, the need for adequate materials and training of local NWMS leaders is a big challenge for the District NWMS Council. All our churches have been active in General Budget giving since the first days of organization. Study about and prayer for our work around the world has helped create the sense of an international family for our Thailand Nazarenes.

Two other important ministries in Thailand are our radio and literature ministries. We've used radio broadcasts from the very beginning, and several of our members at Bangkok First Church had their first contact with the church through them. Presently this ministry is expanding into northern Thailand with special Lahu-speaking programs to be aired from the Philippines. We hope to have Nazarene programs throughout Thailand in the future.

Literature translation and production has continued to be one of our main concerns as the young Thai church has developed. We have been translating the *Manual,* Holiness books, ministerial training materials, NWMS lessons, music, and Sunday School materials. The needs in this area are great, not the least of which is developing trained Thai writers to produce indigenous materials that will not have to be translated.

One of the unique partners in evangelistic outreach for us in Thailand has been Nazarene Compassionate Ministries. NCM has opened many doors for the Church of the Nazarene through projects like building a road to a new hill-tribe village, making it easier to take the gospel there; providing a fertilizer bank, enabling church members to increase their harvests and better provide for their pastors; assisting with an AIDS clinic in Bangkok; or helping to fund the Maetang Tribal Children's Home. Throughout Thailand we have seen compassion evangelism at work.

The Lord has been blessing His work in Thailand. Missionaries from across Thailand, and indeed from across all of Southeast Asia, are working together with national Christians to see the kingdom of God built. It is an immense task, and it is only just begun. Pray with us that the Lord of the harvest will send more workers into the field to help us. Pray too about what the Lord would have you do to advance His kingdom in Thailand and around the world.

10
Sacrifices of Praise

TESTIMONIES OF THAI NAZARENES

Samai Pookrawgta

I WAS BORN IN A SMALL TOWN in northeast Thailand. I married when I was 19 years old, and now I am 31 years old. When I first got married, I had many problems. After my wedding, new problems cropped up in both my family and my husband's family. There were so many financial problems that I had to leave my small daughter with my husband and go to Bangkok to find work. Coming to Bangkok was very difficult. It is a very big city, and when I arrived, I knew no one.

I found work with a Nazarene missionary family. Since I did not know much about Christians, I began to observe the lives of Richard and Jean Knox, to watch what they did. While they were in language study, they attended an English-speaking church on Sundays. However, in October 1990 the first Church of the Nazarene was started near their home. I went with them on the opening Sunday.

I soon found myself riding to church with the Knoxes each week. As I sat under the preaching of our Thai pastor and the missionaries, I began to understand the meaning of being a Christian. Soon I made my own profession of faith in Jesus as my personal Savior. My life began to change for the better immediately, and I began to attend classes to prepare me for baptism.

On Easter Sunday 1991 I was part of the first baptism service held in Bangkok First Church. As I walked down the steps into the baptismal water and took Rev. Knox's hand, I heard the words that he said: "Because of your faith in Jesus Christ as your Lord and Savior, I baptize you in the name of the Father, the Son, and the Holy Spirit." I really did believe in Jesus as my Savior!

Soon I began attending classes to become a church member. It was interesting to learn about the beginning of the Church of the Nazarene and about what the church teaches. As a result, I was in the charter membership class when Bangkok First Church was organized on Pentecost Sunday, 1991.

I continued to grow in the Lord over the next three years and received many spiritual blessings. However, on July 14, 1994, I found a lump in my breast. I went to the doctor for an examination. After the examination, the doctor told me he suspected that I had breast cancer and that I would need surgery. I was in shock, because cancer is a disease everyone fears. When I went home after the doctor's appointment, I sat down and cried. I began to worry so much that I forgot God was there to help me. Suddenly I remembered that God was in my heart and that He said in His Word, "Don't be afraid"—but I was still afraid.

I decided to go to another doctor for a second opinion. He also suspected cancer and proceeded to do a biopsy. The doctor was very surprised to find on further examination that there was no cancer. I was so relieved. I am so glad that Jesus is my Savior.

❋ ❋ ❋

Jasuh Jana (as told by Samuel Yangmi)

The Lahu tribes of northern Thailand are among the many worldwide tribal groups who are still waiting for the Creator of the universe to reveal himself. In the meantime, they still believe that animal sacrifice can save them from the bad things that happen to them. A shaman or a witch doctor does most of the spiritual work for the villagers. He is powerful and highly regarded as the man who deals with the spiritual world and communicates with evil spirits, who put great fear in and demands on the people.

Jasuh was one of those witch doctors. Not only did he become one by succession from another witch doctor, but the evil spirits came upon him. He had the reputation of being a powerful witch doctor. However, deep in Jasuh's heart he knew that one day the real God would reveal himself to him.

One day as Jasuh sat on his bamboo house porch overlooking the Mae Kok River, he saw a strange vision upon the water. Two men dressed in white were walking upon the water going downstream. They looked at Jasuh and told him that the true God was planning to visit him, and that when He came, Jasuh should receive Him.

This vision was very puzzling to Jasuh, but he kept it to himself. Jasuh recalls that he was totally in control of himself when he saw the vision. He was not drunk or high on opium. To be a real witch doctor, he had to keep his body pure and completely off any habit-forming substance. There were also many things he had to do to keep evil spirits with him. Sometimes just the thought of doing bad could cause the spirits to leave. Then Jasuh would be required to sacrifice animals to call back the spirits when he had to do his priestly duty.

Not long after this vision, one of our evangelists who was assigned to a village farther down the river had to spend the night at Jasuh's village. According to Lahu custom, the evangelist was required to look for the headman's house or the village witch doctor. The evangelist came to Jasuh's house, and Jasuh greeted him and welcomed him into his home. After a good meal, the evangelist took out a Viewmaster set that I [Samuel Yangmi] had given him. The set had been purchased from Vacation Bible School funds given by a Sunday School class in Smithville, Missouri.

The picture in the Viewmaster was none other than from the story of Moses. To Jasuh's surprise, the picture was identical to the men he saw in his vision! Putting down the Viewmaster, Jasuh told the evangelist, "I have been waiting for this message of the true God. I was instructed to receive your message. What must I do to receive God?"

The evangelist had never experienced such a response from a witch doctor. He was so surprised at Jasuh's response that he changed his itinerary for the next day. Instead of going downstream, he asked if he could stay and teach Jasuh. I said, "Certainly—you must change your plans if God is calling you to stay." After three months, Jasuh and his household came to accept Christ. I had the great honor of going to his house and burning all the evil spirit shelves in his home at the river's shore. Jasuh was the first Red Lahu baptized in northern Thailand.

Jasuh Jana, with Samuel Yangmi, removing his "spirit shelf."

Persecution soon began as the non-Christian family members began to blame Jasuh for every sickness and unexplainable problem in the village. A mercenary hit man came and told Jasuh that there was a $200 bounty on his head. The man gave Jasuh a date by which he had to pay the money, or the hit man would accept the contract and come to kill him.

Jasuh consulted with the evangelist and asked me for money. I didn't have that much money on hand, so I went to other missionaries, collecting donations enough to pay for Jasuh's life. Soon after the money was paid, Jasuh and his family moved into a Christian village. There he learned to read and write Lahu. Occasionally, when the local pastor had to be gone on Sunday, Jasuh would take over and give his testimony. He became a mature Christian within five to seven years.

About nine years after Jasuh's conversion, I was praying for an evangelist for the Pa Yang village. Jasuh's name came into my mind. I thought, "Why not Jasuh, the first Red Lahu convert and a former witch doctor?" When I asked Jasuh of his calling, he had an amazing testimony. He said that years ago when the death sentence was on his head, he had told God that if he survived, he would give his life to Him in full-time service. I had long forgotten the $200 that had saved Jasuh's life from the hit man. God had given me the opportunity to have a small part in helping Jasuh not only to be rescued from the hit man but also to become a Christian leader among his people.

In September 1994 a revival broke out in Pa Yang, Jasuh's village. Through the influence of visits from a Work and Witness team from the Intermountain District and the Korea Central District NWMS Council, much prayer was offered to the Lord for this village. As a result, many families began turning from animism and turning to the Lord. In October 1994 the village headman and his wife were baptized, and the church continued to grow.

Soon the small bamboo church had to be expanded. However, eventually this, too, proved inadequate for the growing church family. Plans were made for a Work and Witness team to build an adequate place of worship for Pa Yang. In March 1996 a Work and Witness team from Nampa, Idaho, College Church was able to come and complete this project. Jasuh was so very proud when that building was dedicated two months later.

Pa Yang Church of the Nazarene

Today Jasuh continues as the pastor in Pa Yang and faithfully serves Christ among his own people. Every night it is not unusual to find Jasuh visiting in village homes and praying with the families in order to encourage them to stand strong against the forces of evil. Lives continue to be changed under his leadership. Young people are learning music. Adults are learning how to read and write. And new villages are beginning to open to the gospel because of the ministry of Jasuh.

One of the most unique things about Jasuh is his humble, soft-spoken, gentle personality. He is always asking older pastors to teach him more hymns so that he can teach his people. He is a praying pastor. He prays in each member's home, asking God to heal the sick and protect each family from evil spirits.

Jasuh tells us that there are actually some similarities between his old life as a witch doctor under the power of the evil spirits and his new life under the power of the Holy Spirit. However, the main difference is that under the old system it was impossible to maintain a pure enough life to keep the spirits happy. Today in Christ there is a fullness and the consistent companionship of the Holy Spirit that lives in him and gives him peace of mind with God on a daily basis. Jasuh is an ordinary man doing extraordinary work and service for God's kingdom in Thailand among his own people, whom he dearly loves.

* * *

Wiboon Chevawattana

My father passed away when I was about 12 years old. From then on I began to search for the love that a child needs from his dad. I thought the love of my father had totally gone from my life. I lived an unhappy life for 12 more years. This was a critical period of my life, because I was a teenager. I tried doing many crazy things to fill up the hole in my heart, but I still couldn't find the love I needed. Many times I felt inferior for having no dad as other people had.

During this time my family lived in a section of Bangkok called Chinatown. There was a Christian family who lived next door, and I was interested in their lives. I wondered what caused them to be so happy.

When I found out that they went to church each Sunday, I thought that church must be a good place to go and that perhaps I could find happiness there. I started going to church with them and also attended Sunday School each week. I learned a lot about God, Jesus, and the Holy Spirit. After attending the church for one year, I realized that God loved me, and His love was eternal. I decided to be baptized in 1981, when I was 24 years old. I have been a Christian since that day. I am no longer the master of my own life, but God is.

When I became a Christian, my life started to gradually change. Initially, my mother and sisters were not happy with me becoming a Christian, because they knew that Christians do not worship evil or ancestral spirits. Since I am Chinese, worshiping our ancestors is an important spiritual duty. However, my mother and sisters liked the changes they began to see in me after I became a Christian. They said I looked much happier than I had looked before. I shared my testimony with them and told them how God had changed me.

In 1992 I moved from Chinatown to the east side of Bangkok. Since my former church was such a long way from my new house, I began to look around my neighborhood for another local church where I could attend. After visiting several, I found a small church that called itself the Church of the Nazarene. It was a new church with much challenge ahead and a good opportunity for growth. I wanted to be a part of its future.

After talking this over with the Lord, I decided to give myself to helping in this church ministry. I immediately found that they needed an English/Thai translator, and I volunteered for the job. I consider this my personal ministry for the Lord each Sunday. I have also become involved in some literature translation this past year. In 1994 I was elected the local NWMS president and chosen to assist Mrs. Rachel McCarty as the district NWMS vice president.

I enjoy learning about the work of the Church of the Nazarene worldwide, as well as introducing our international family to our Thai Nazarenes. I thank God that when I moved to a new location, I also found a new church family. How great is God's love for me! It is exciting to serve Him!

✳ ✳ ✳

Warnnachai and Veeranya Donchan
(as told by Jean Knox)

Warnnachai Donchan is a Thai from one of the southern provinces of Thailand. He came to Bangkok looking for work and a college education. Due to several problems in his life, Warnnachai, known as "Don," became so distraught that he contemplated committing suicide. His Buddhist background provided him no help in solving his problems. At this critical moment a faithful Christian found Don and ministered to him. The friend presented the gospel, and Don's life miraculously changed as he accepted Jesus as his personal Savior.

When the McCartys and Knoxes arrived in Thailand in 1989, Don became a key player in church planting efforts. By that time he had been nurtured and discipled and had become a strong Christian with the gift of evangelism. Don's evangelistic heart was always reaching out to his own people, sharing God's Word, praying with them, and helping them however he could. Don and his contacts with Thai friends and businessmen were of great assistance to the Nazarene missionaries in obtaining the Bangkapi building, which would house Bangkok First Church of the Nazarene. His evangelistic skills assisted the missionaries in introducing new Thai believers to the Church of the Nazarene.

On January 20, 1991, Don married Veeranya (known as Vee), a lovely Chinese Christian. Vee became our district office secretary. She and Don were expecting their first child when tragedy struck. On June 15, 1992, Vee suffered an aneurysm. She was in her sixth month of pregnancy, and the original prognosis was very poor. She was in a coma for two weeks. There was medical concern for both her and the baby.

The NWMS Prayer Mobilization Line was notified. Soon thousands of Nazarenes all over the world were praying for Vee. Their prayers were answered when after two weeks of a comatose state, Vee awoke and suffered few side effects from the aneurysm. September 28, 1992, was a day of victory as Piyapawn, a beautiful healthy daughter, arrived to be greeted by proud parents. Piyapawn is almost five years old now. She is a bright, playful girl who loves to explore her environment.

Don has started a new business in Bangkok, providing security officers for Thai businesses. His training for his workers includes sharing the gospel with them. He is leading many of them to Christ and is also acquainting them with Bangkok First Church.

Last year Vee experienced a difficult time with her health. The Thai doctors believe there may be additional problems due to the aneurysm that caused her unusual symptoms. However, through the prayers of her friends at Bangkok First Church

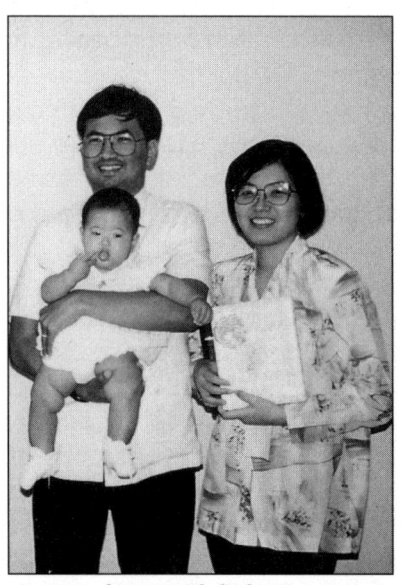

Don and Vee with little Piyapawn

and some new medicine, she has improved. She continues to gain strength and is now able to spend more time with her husband and precious daughter.

As you finish reading this chapter and this book on Nazarene work in Thailand, would you pause to pray for Vee? Pray for her health to be completely restored. Pray for Don as he shares his spiritual gift of evangelism with Thais who need to know Jesus. Pray for little Piyapawn, that she will have the privilege of being our first second-generation Nazarene in Thailand and that there will be many more to come.